What Is the Story of Jurassic Park?

by Jim Gigliotti

illustrated by Dede Putra

Penguin Workshop

PENGUIN WORKSHOP
An imprint of Penguin Random House LLC, New York

First published in the United States of America by Penguin Workshop,
an imprint of Penguin Random House LLC, New York, 2023

Visit us online at penguinrandomhouse.com.

Library of Congress Cataloging-in-Publication Data is available.

Printed in the United States of America

ISBN 9780593383483 (paperback)   10 9 8 7 6 5 4 3 2 1 WOR
ISBN 9780593386910 (library binding)   10 9 8 7 6 5 4 3 2 1 WOR

Contents

What Is the Story of Jurassic World?

One day in the late 1980s, when author Michael Crichton and his wife were preparing for the birth of their first child, the famous writer bought a stuffed dinosaur. Then he bought another. And another. And still another. He bought so many stuffed dinosaurs, in fact, that his wife finally stopped him and said, "Why is this happening?"

It was happening because Michael Crichton had loved dinosaurs ever since he was young. He knew that many other children felt the same way. And he decided right then that he would write a book with dinosaurs in it.

The book, which reached stores in November 1990, was called *Jurassic Park*.

The idea behind Crichton's story went like this: Sixty-five million years ago, a mosquito landed on a dinosaur. The mosquito bit the dinosaur, sucking a small amount of blood from the animal, then buzzed off to rest on a tree. But the mosquito was caught in a sticky, sap-like substance on the tree called resin. The insect couldn't escape, and it died. After that, the resin expanded to surround the dead insect and hardened into amber. So the insect was perfectly preserved in amber.

The story then jumped ahead to the late twentieth century, when workers on a remote island in Central America dug up that same piece of amber. A scientist inserted a probe into the amber and removed the mosquito blood, which contained the dinosaur blood that the insect had sucked. The scientist took the genetic building blocks from the dinosaur blood and re-created the long-extinct creature.

A businessman saw an opportunity in this amazing technology. He hired scientists to create several different species of dinosaurs, then bought the Central American island and built a theme park where the animals could live and people could visit them.

The dinosaurs in Michael Crichton's story weren't described as just pictures in a book or bones in a museum. Visitors to the theme park could see and hear the incredible living creatures for themselves. Of course, many safety precautions were put in place, but things didn't go exactly as planned. It was the beginning of an exciting—and terrifying—adventure tale.

In 1993, Universal Pictures produced *Jurassic Park*, the first of several movies based on Crichton's book. The combination of realistic science, awe-inspiring dinosaurs, and a thrilling

story made the film the biggest blockbuster up to that time in movie history and launched one of the most successful franchises of all time. Since then, Michael Crichton's book *Jurassic Park* has grown into Jurassic World—an entire world of movies, books, games, theme park encounters, and more. Let's dig into the story of Jurassic World!

CHAPTER 1
The Jurassic Age

Why are so many people fascinated by dinosaurs?

A paleontologist (say: PAY-lee-on-TAH-lo-jist) named Stephen Jay Gould once famously said it is because they are "big, fierce, and extinct." A paleontologist is a scientist who studies fossils to learn about ancient life forms. Fossils are any traces of plant or animal life—like the bones or teeth of a dinosaur—

that have been preserved in the earth's crust. Gould's quote meant that even though many dinosaurs might have been huge, scary animals, we aren't afraid of them because they don't exist anymore. They last roamed the earth about sixty-five million years ago.

It is true that many dinosaurs were big. Scientists estimate the dinosaur *Argentinosaurus* (say: ar-jen-TEEN-uh-SORE-us) was the largest land animal ever. They believe the four-legged

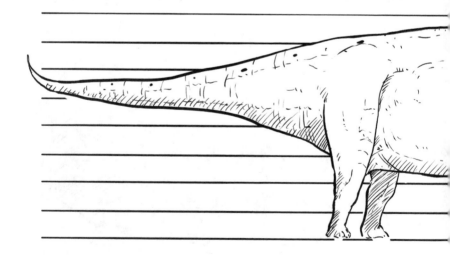

giant was as long as 130 feet and as tall as 65 feet. Not many animals were as fierce as *Tyrannosaurus rex* (say: tu-RAN-uh-SORE-us REX). *T. rex*, as it also is known, could bite with a force of eight to ten thousand pounds per square inch. That's more than double the bite of a saltwater crocodile, which has the most powerful bite of any animal alive today, and more than fifty times the bite of a human!

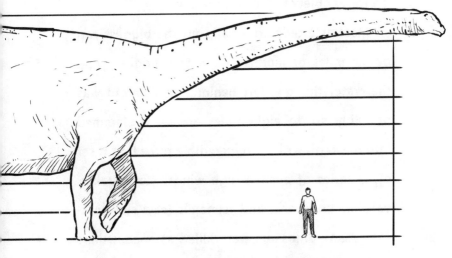

Argentinosaurus

Human

What Killed Off the Dinosaurs?

Why did dinosaurs go extinct? The answer is, nobody knows for sure. After all, no human was around sixty-five million years ago to keep records! But scientists have a pretty good clue from a giant crater—a bowl-shaped impression in the earth—found underneath the Yucatán Peninsula in Mexico in the 1990s. They believe the crater indicates that a giant asteroid slammed into the earth. An asteroid is a rocky object that orbits the sun.

Most asteroids are small, but the biggest can be 125 miles or more in diameter! Judging from the crater this one left behind, the asteroid was probably six to eight miles across. It slammed into the earth with such incredible force that it set off a series of events: high winds, earthquakes, volcanic eruptions, and tsunamis (say: sue-NAM-ees). Many dinosaurs were killed at once. Others

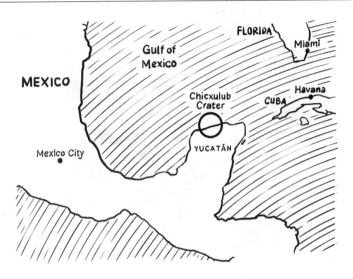

Chicxulub Crater, Yucatán, Mexico

eventually died when pollution and smoke from the impact blocked out the sun, causing temperatures to drop and impacting plant life and the food supply.

It wasn't just dinosaurs that felt the impact of the asteroid and its disastrous effects. Scientists believe the event wiped out three-quarters of all the prehistoric animal life on Earth.

Microraptor

And yet . . . not all dinosaurs were big. *Microraptor* (say: MY-cro-RAP-tor) measured only a couple of feet from head to tail and weighed just two pounds. Not all dinosaurs were fierce, either. Many were herbivores, or plant eaters. And although nonflying dinosaurs are also extinct, modern birds are their direct ancestors and are sometimes called living dinosaurs.

Although their reputation for being "big, fierce, and extinct" is among the reasons that people are fascinated by dinosaurs, it isn't the only one. We're also interested because we are curious. What would it be like to see a dinosaur? We can go to the zoo and see a giraffe or an alligator or a gorilla. But no person has ever seen a real, live dinosaur.

The first dinosaurs inhabited the earth about 235 million years ago, and for 56 million years—from about 201 million years ago to 145 million years ago—they were the world's dominant creatures. This was the Jurassic Period, the geological stretch of time from which the Jurassic World franchise takes its name.

Dinosaurs lived on almost every part of the earth. That's because when dinosaurs first were alive, the earth's land was connected in one large mass called Pangaea (say: pan-JEE-uh). During the Jurassic Period, Pangaea began to split into separate land masses, which eventually became the continents that exist today. That separation process is called continental drift.

Geologic Time

Scientists divide Earth's history into several categories. Among them are periods, which are part of larger time frames called eras. The first dinosaurs appeared in the Triassic Period, which is part of the Mesozoic (say: mez-uh-ZOH-ick) Era. The Jurassic Period followed the Triassic Period in the same era.

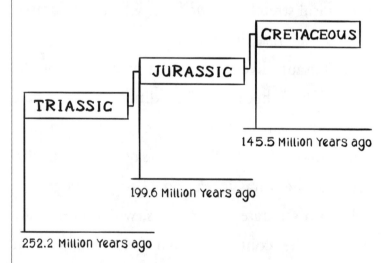

Mesozoic Era

Dinosaurs such as the *Brachiosaurus* (say: BRAK-ee-oh-SORE-us) and *Allosaurus* (say: AL-oh-SORE-us)—featured in the Jurassic World movies—roamed the earth during the Jurassic Period. Others in the movies, such as the *Tyrannosaurus rex* and *Triceratops* (say: try-SER-uh-tops), came later, during the Cretaceous (say: cree-TAY-shush) Period of the Mesozoic Era.

Human beings didn't arrive until about three hundred thousand years ago, long after dinosaurs were gone. We live in the Quaternary (say: kwaa-TUR-neh-ree) Period in the Cenozoic (say: see-nuh-ZOH-ick) Era.

Pangaea

One reason scientists know about continental drift is because dinosaur fossils found on the eastern side of South America, for instance, are similar to ones found on the western side of Africa, across the Atlantic Ocean. So scientists believe that those areas of land were once connected.

Dinosaur fossils became buried in the earth over millions of years. A dinosaur's body, for example, may have sunk into the mud after it died. Its skin and other soft tissues soon decayed, leaving the bones behind in the mud. Over millions of years, sand, dirt, and minerals mixed with the mud and turned it into rock well below the earth's surface. Over millions more years, wind and rain eroded the surface and exposed the rock, enabling paleontologists to discover bones that had been encased in hard rock as fossils.

In the late 1700s, French zoologist Georges Cuvier, who is sometimes called the father of paleontology, identified such fossil bones as coming from extinct animals. In 1842, these animals got their name when British paleontologist Richard Owen took the Greek words meaning

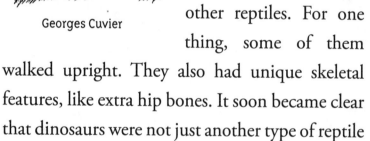

Georges Cuvier

"fearfully great" (*deinos*) and "lizard" (*sauros*) and gave them the name *dinosauria*. From that came the word *dinosaurs*.

Richard Owen referred to them as lizards, but they were different from other reptiles. For one thing, some of them walked upright. They also had unique skeletal features, like extra hip bones. It soon became clear that dinosaurs were not just another type of reptile or other animal—they were their own branch in the tree of life.

CHAPTER 2
Novel Beginnings

A little more than a decade after giving dinosaurs their name, Richard Owen convinced the directors of the Crystal Palace Park in London, England, to include life-size sculptures of them in an outdoor exhibit of extinct animals. The dinosaur sculptures were unveiled in 1854.

Richard Owen

As it turned out, the depictions of the dinosaurs were mostly wrong. Then again, Owen and Benjamin Waterhouse Hawkins, the man who made the sculptures, didn't have much information to go on. At that time, only three dinosaur species had been identified, and no complete skeleton for any species had been found. So even though Owen and Hawkins used the most current scientific knowledge available to them, they still had to do a lot of guessing.

For most people, the Crystal Palace Park dinosaurs marked the first time they had ever seen any images of this recently discovered life-form. And because the sculptures looked like lazy, overgrown lizards, they helped create the idea that dinosaurs were huge, slow animals.

Only a few years later, in 1858, the first full dinosaur skeleton, a *Hadrosaurus*, was unearthed in the United States, in Haddonfield, New Jersey. Soon, more and more dinosaur species were identified—and more realistic representations of dinosaurs began appearing in popular culture outlets.

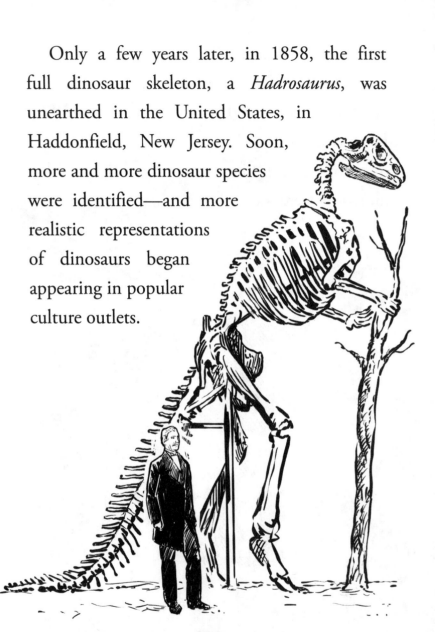

Full *Hadrosaurus* skeleton, found in 1858

By the early twentieth century, the creatures were featured in toys, books, games, comics, and cartoons. They even started appearing in motion pictures as early as 1905. No copies of that year's short film *Prehistoric Peeps* still exist, but the "animals" in it were simply actors dressed up in dinosaur costumes.

Other early attempts at showing dinosaurs on the movie screen were just as silly. Sometimes, a moviemaker might film a common lizard from really close to make it look big. Sometimes the lizard had cardboard "plates" attached to make it look like a stegosaurus (say: STEG-oh-SORE-us). Other times, as in 1914's *Brute Force*, an alligator was made to look like a dinosaur.

By the time the movie *The Lost World* was released in 1925, dinosaurs were created on the big screen by using a stop-motion animation technique with toy animals. To achieve the desired effect, many still photos are taken of an object, like a small toy dinosaur; the images are moved slightly after each individual photo. When they are put together, the illusion of motion results. But the movement often looks awkward and not realistic.

The Lost World, which featured an allosaurus, a brachiosaur, a brontosaurus (say: BRON-tuh-SORE-us), a triceratops, and more dinosaurs, was based on a book of the same name written by Sir Arthur Conan Doyle that was published in 1912. It was an adventure story about a group of explorers led by a man named Professor Challenger. The explorers found prehistoric animals still living in South America. Conan Doyle, the creator of Sherlock Holmes, wanted to make an adventure hero as popular as his fictional detective star. While Professor Challenger never became as well-known as Sherlock Holmes, *The Lost World* gained a following of readers over the years, including a young boy living in Roslyn, New York, in the 1950s named Michael Crichton.

Michael Crichton, who was born in Chicago in 1942, was still a youngster when *The Lost World* sparked his imagination about dinosaurs. Although Crichton grew up wanting to be a writer, he graduated from Harvard in 1962 with a degree in biological anthropology and later enrolled in medical school at the university.

Arthur Conan Doyle (1859–1930)

Arthur Conan Doyle was a writer and physician most known for creating the fictional detective Sherlock Holmes.

Born in Edinburgh (say: ED-in-bruh), Scotland, Conan Doyle got his storytelling skills from his mother, Mary. "The vivid stories she would tell me stand out so clearly that they obscure the real facts of my life," he once wrote.

After graduating from the University of Edinburgh with a degree in medicine in 1881, Conan Doyle tried to balance his medical practice with writing. He eventually left his career as a doctor behind to become a full-time writer. His character Sherlock Holmes debuted in 1887 and was based on one of his professors in medical school.

Conan Doyle received the title *Sir* after he was knighted by King Edward VII in 1902 for his work as a volunteer doctor during the Second Boer War in South Africa.

But writing remained Crichton's passion, and he published several novels under different names while still in medical school. The first book published under his own name was *The Andromeda Strain* in 1969, the same year he graduated from medical school.

Crichton's education at Harvard helped him write stories that were often based on scientific ideas. *The Andromeda Strain*, for instance, was a thriller about a microscopic organism that was brought to a town in Arizona by a US military satellite. The organism was accidentally released, killing many people.

In the late 1980s, Crichton became concerned about the growing field of genetic engineering—making changes to the genetic code of an animal or plant to create a man-made result. One example that Crichton noted was scientists growing square tree trunks to make them easier for loggers to cut. Another was producing trout that were pale in color to make them easier for fishermen to see. He believed it was foolish to interfere with nature in such ways.

Crichton combined his love of dinosaurs with his concerns about genetic engineering to write the novel *Jurassic Park*, which was published in 1990. He said he wanted to "take something that might seem like a good idea [a dinosaur theme park] and show why it might *not* be a good idea." So, he began the novel with a real-life scientific technique: removing blood from an insect preserved in amber to create living dinosaurs.

Jurassic Park was an instant hit. The book spent twelve weeks on the best seller list in the early 1990s. By summer 1993, nine million copies of the novel were in print. Even before *Jurassic Park* reached bookshelves, Universal Pictures had recognized its movie potential. It outbid several competitors for the film rights to the book.

CHAPTER 3
Clever Girl

Jurassic Park, which reached theaters in June 1993, was a groundbreaking movie directed by Steven Spielberg.

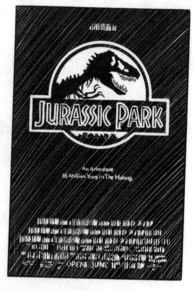

It featured new ways of showing dinosaurs on-screen that were far beyond what any other dinosaur movie had ever done. It also helped change the way many people think about dinosaurs. And audiences went to see *Jurassic Park* just because it was fun!

With scary, realistic dinosaurs—and lots of

action, adventure, and suspense—*Jurassic Park* was unlike any other film that had come before it. And moviegoers of all ages went to see *Jurassic Park* in record numbers. In its first three days, the movie made more money in ticket sales ($47 million) than any other movie ever had on its opening weekend. After only nine days, it had made more than $100 million. It soon passed *E.T. the Extra-Terrestrial* (which was also directed by Spielberg) for the most money ever in ticket sales—and it would go on to make more than a billion dollars around the globe! Not bad for a movie that had cost about $65 million to make.

Michael Crichton helped write the screenplay for the film *Jurassic Park*. Many elements of the screenplay were the same as the storyline for his book, beginning with the core idea of dinosaur DNA being extracted from a mosquito encased in amber.

In the movie, just as in the book, the scientist and businessman Dr. John Hammond built a dinosaur theme park. Lab-created dinosaurs roamed the park for the entertainment of visitors. Hammond was the owner of InGen Corporation. His park was located on Isla Nublar,

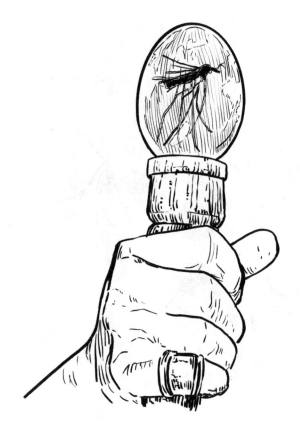

a small island about 120 miles west of Costa Rica. Park dinosaurs ranged from the large but nonthreatening *Brachiosaurus* and *Triceratops* to the terrifying *Tyrannosaurus rex* and *Velociraptor* (say: veh-LA-suh-RAP-tor) and others.

Jurassic Park was not yet open to the public as

a tourist attraction when game warden Robert Muldoon and some park workers were moving a velociraptor to its holding pen one night. The raptor reached out with a supersharp claw and killed one of the workers.

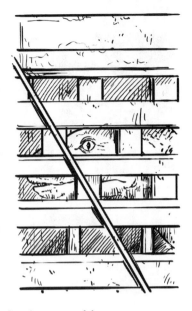

That made some of the park's investors (people who supply money to help a business get started in return for a share of the profits) very nervous. The investors started to wonder whether the park was safe enough for visitors. So, before Jurassic Park could officially open, Hammond needed experts to approve the island's safety. He invited Dr. Alan Grant (a paleontologist played by the actor Sam Neill), Dr. Ellie Sattler (a paleobotanist played by Laura

Dern), and Dr. Ian Malcolm (a mathematician played by Jeff Goldblum) to explore the park.

Hammond took his visitors around the island. He showed them the concrete moats, tracking system, electrified fences, and other safety features. But what really got their attention, of course, were the dinosaurs. The first time

Grant and Sattler saw a dinosaur, a brachiosaur, they were overwhelmed with delight. After all, dinosaurs were their life's work. But the closest they had ever come to a dinosaur were the bones

and fossils they would uncover at a dig site.

Hammond's two grandchildren joined the experts on the island and were awed by the sight of the dinosaurs, too. But things began to go wrong. The man who designed the park's computer system, Dennis Nedry, got greedy. He wanted more money than Hammond was paying him. So he tried to steal dinosaur embryos—early-stage unhatched dinosaurs created in the laboratory— and sell them to one of InGen's competitors.

To make his plan work, Nedry had to turn

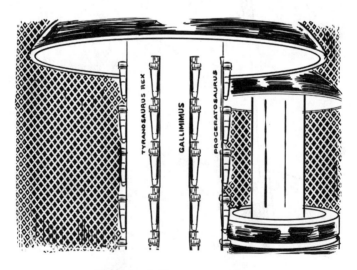

Display of dinosaur embryos

off Jurassic Park's electrical systems for just a few minutes. But he crashed his car during a storm and was killed by a dilophosaur (say: die-LOAF-oh-sore). With all the electrical systems off for an extended time, the dinosaurs broke out of their enclosures and put all the visitors at risk.

Director Steven Spielberg created an intense atmosphere of suspense that kept viewers on the edge of their seats. The movie built to an exciting conclusion that featured a battle between two velociraptors and a *T. rex*.

Those dinosaurs, and the others in *Jurassic
Park*, were frighteningly realistic. Some were
animatronic, which means they were electronically

controlled robotic figures. And some were CGI, which means they were computer-generated images.

How to Make a Movie Dinosaur

Steven Spielberg, the director of *Jurassic Park*, knew the dinosaurs were the real stars of his movie. He set out to create the most terrifying and realistic dinosaurs ever seen on film.

The dinosaurs in certain scenes—like when a herd of stampeding *Gallimimus* (say: gal-lee-MIME-us) runs from a predator—were created with computer-generated images. But Spielberg wanted the *T. rex* that terrorized Dr. John Hammond's visitors to be as close to the real thing as possible! So he hired Stan Winston Studio to create a giant *T. rex* for *Jurassic Park*.

They began with what looked like a wood-and-steel cage in the shape of a dinosaur. It housed a complicated mechanical system that controlled the *T. rex*'s movements. The cage was then covered with chicken wire that could be bent and shaped as desired. That form was covered by fiberglass and layers of clay sculpted into a dinosaur with accurate details including its wrinkles and skin texture. When it was completed, the robotic *T. rex* was twenty feet tall. It weighed nine thousand pounds.

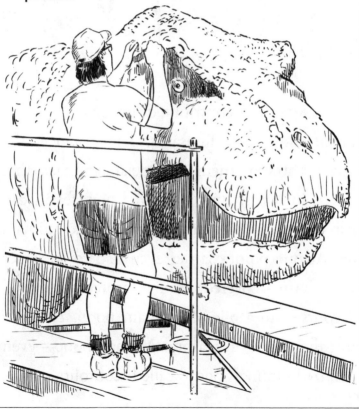

Jurassic Park contributed to many people's understanding of dinosaurs. For instance, the movie showed them as social animals that moved in herds. And it showed how fossils can help scientists reconstruct a prehistoric animal's life. At one point, Sattler even had to stick her whole arm—covered with a protective sleeve, of course—in a pile of dinosaur poop. *Ewwww!* But there was a reason: Animal poop—even fossilized animal poop called coprolite—gives scientists clues about an animal's health and eating habits.

But perhaps *Jurassic Park* was most influential in how it changed the way we think about dinosaurs. Before that movie, almost everyone considered dinosaurs to be slow-moving and unintelligent. *Jurassic Park* showed many of them to be flexible jumpers, fast runners—and smart. This was best illustrated when Muldoon began tracking a raptor to protect Sattler, who was trying to restart the park's electrical systems. Muldoon was alert and ready. He was a skilled hunter.

And he knew very well how dangerous, and cunning, raptors could be. "They show extraordinary intelligence," he said at one point in the movie, "even problem-solving intelligence."

He was aiming at a raptor with a tranquilizer gun when he realized he had been outsmarted by her. The raptor had served as a decoy so

another could move in on Muldoon unnoticed. "Clever girl," Muldoon said admiringly—just as it dawned on him that he was about to be eaten. Although Muldoon didn't make it out alive, Hammond, his grandchildren, and the experts all did. But Hammond's Jurassic Park never opened as a theme park.

CHAPTER 4
Life Finds a Way

Even while the original *Jurassic Park* movie was still in theaters, engineers began working on a theme park thrill ride for Universal Studios Hollywood. Riders traveled along a river that looked as if it came straight out of the film. Of course, things hadn't gone well for visitors in *Jurassic Park*. Not to worry, a recording of Dr. John Hammond told people as they waited in line for Jurassic Park: The Ride, which opened to the public in 1996. "We had a few problems in Costa Rica," he said, "but have all the bugs worked out now."

The riders boarded a boat. "Welcome to Jurassic Park!" a narrator boomed as the movie's theme music played. The raft passed along a river, through a rainforest built with more than one thousand trees and seven thousand shrubs, plants, and flowers. The raft glided pleasantly past a fifty-foot-tall, plant-eating ultrasaurus; a psittacosaurus (say: si-tak-oh-SORE-us); and gently cascading waterfalls. Everything seemed to be going fine.

But then, an alert sounded! A parasaurolophus (say: pa-ra-SORE-oh-LOH-fus) nudged the raft, sending it toward a restricted area that contained raptors. Horns sounded, red lights flashed. A dilophosaur spit its venom—just water, really—at the raft, which began a steep incline toward a genetics laboratory. A velociraptor menacingly threatened the riders. At the top of the climb, a *T. rex*! It opened its huge jaws wide,

ready to devour the riders. The raft made a narrow escape by way of a terrifying drop to a splashdown below.

It was an exciting and popular attraction. Riders felt like they were in a scene from the movie *Jurassic Park*. Indeed, the dinosaurs featured in the ride were created using some of the same technology that went into making the dinosaurs in the movie. Some of the ride's dinosaurs cost more than a million dollars to make.

Jurassic Park: The Ride closed in 2018 and was replaced by a new Jurassic World: The Ride one year later. By then, Michael Crichton had written *The Lost World*, a sequel to the original *Jurassic Park* novel. The title of the 1995 book was a tribute to the 1912 novel of the same title by Sir Arthur Conan Doyle that Crichton had enjoyed as a youngster. Crichton's book was adapted into the movie *The Lost World: Jurassic Park* in 1997. Dr. John Hammond and

Dr. Ian Malcolm were returning characters from the first film. The sequel took place on Isla Sorna, eighty-seven miles southwest of Isla Nublar, four years after the events of the first movie. By then,

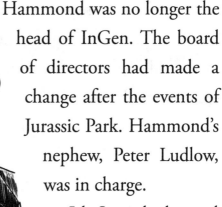

Peter Ludlow

Hammond was no longer the head of InGen. The board of directors had made a change after the events of Jurassic Park. Hammond's nephew, Peter Ludlow, was in charge.

Isla Sorna had served as a second site for InGen's experiments. All the animals created by InGen were supposed to be female. Without males present, they were unable to have babies. But, as Hammond reminded Malcolm of his own words from the first movie, "Life finds a way."

Left on their own after the failure of the

theme park in the first movie, the animals on Isla Sorna found a way. They reproduced, and their population grew. Hammond wanted to know exactly what dinosaurs, and how many of them, were living on the island. He was no longer interested in making money by showing off the dinosaurs, but instead only in preserving their environment. He hired a paleontologist, an equipment expert, and a photographer, and he wanted Malcolm to join them.

At first, Malcolm wanted no part of the idea. After all, he was there when all the trouble started in the original *Jurassic Park* movie. But Malcolm reconsidered when he found out that the paleontologist Hammond hired was Dr. Sarah Harding. She was Malcolm's girlfriend and had already begun working on the island.

Malcolm traveled to Isla Sorna. But once he was there, several complications quickly developed. For one, his thirteen-year-old daughter, Kelly, had snuck on board and traveled with him. For another, Ludlow had hired a group of men to capture the dinosaurs and take them to the United States. He wanted to open a Jurassic Park in San Diego, California. But the biggest danger came when Malcolm, Harding, and the photographer, Nick Van Owen, rescued a baby *T. rex* from the men trying to take the dinosaurs to San Diego. They did a good deed by mending the baby's broken leg—but its parents didn't know that! They knew only that their baby was in the hands of strangers.

The two adult—and very large—*T. rexes* went after the group. They killed the equipment expert, Eddie Carr. The others escaped.

The incident showed that these dinosaurs were caring parents. For a long time, real-life scientists thought that the adults left their offspring to fend for themselves. Now they believe that the lack of many young *T. rex* fossils indicates

that they were nurtured and cared for beyond birth.

In the end, Ludlow's men eventually captured the adult male *T. rex* and its baby, and they took them to San Diego aboard a ship. But the ship crashed into a dock in California with disastrous consequences. The *T. rex* and its baby were eventually sent back to Isla Sorna.

CHAPTER 5
The Best Intentions

Four years after *The Lost World: Jurassic Park* premiered in 1997, *Jurassic Park III*—also set on Isla Sorna—was released. One of the most memorable scenes in that 2001 film took place in the Aviary, which is a place that houses birds. This Aviary also contained flying reptiles called pteranodons (say: ter-AHN-oh-dawns).

Pteranodon

Modern birds evolved from two-legged, meat-eating dinosaurs called theropods—the same branch of the family tree that also produced *Tyrannosaurus rex*. Yes, dinosaurs have been extinct for sixty-five million years. But because of their ancestry, birds are sometimes called living dinosaurs. And scientists now classify dinosaurs as non-avian dinosaurs (which are extinct) and avian dinosaurs (living birds).

Imagine small dinosaurs, like mini raptors, covered in feathers. Picture sharp teeth in their mouths. Some scientists believe early birds evolved from such creatures. Over time, many birds lost their teeth and developed beaks. Scientists are still trying to figure out exactly why that was, but it likely had something to do with a changing diet as birds became plant eaters.

The earliest known bird was the archaeopteryx (say: ar-kee-OP-tur-ix). It first lived about 150 million years ago. An archaeopteryx had sharp teeth and a bony tail, like a dinosaur. It had feathers and wings, like a bird. It could fly, although scientists still aren't sure how well.

Archaeopteryx

Archaeopteryx was a dinosaur. But other flying reptiles that looked like birds were not. These were pterosaurs (say: TARE-oh-sores). The name means "winged lizards." Even though pterosaurs weren't technically dinosaurs, they were closely related on the family tree. Sound confusing? The reason has to do with physical differences in their bones. That's one way scientists classify animals. Pterosaurs included *Pteranodon*, *Preondactylus* (say: pree-ahn-DACK-til-us), *Quetzalcoatlus* (say: KET-zel-ko-WAT-lus), and other creatures.

Quetzalcoatlus

Why Did Birds Survive Extinction?

When most of the prehistoric animal population, including dinosaurs, was wiped out some sixty-five million years ago, beaked, toothless birds survived. Why?

These birds were small and didn't need as much food to live. With food being scarce, that wasn't as big a problem for them as it was for, say, a large brachiosaur. The type of food that beaked birds ate

helped, too. They didn't need big, leafy plants or other animals as prey. Small seeds or insects often were enough. And, of course, birds were a lot more mobile than lumbering dinosaurs. They could fly to new areas in search of food and sunlight, or to move away from predators and poor air quality.

Pteranodons lived between eighty-one and one hundred million years ago, in the Cretaceous Period. They had a long neck; a long, toothless beak; and wide wings. Pteranodons appeared in *Jurassic Park III*. The pteranodons on Isla Sorna were housed in the giant Aviary, which was enclosed by a huge, steel cage.

The story of *Jurassic Park III* began when a divorced couple, Amanda and Paul Kirby, tricked Dr. Alan Grant into returning to Isla Sorna to search for their twelve-year-old son, Eric. He had gone missing on the island after a parasailing accident with Amanda's boyfriend, who was killed. Grant brought along Billy Brennan, an associate professor of paleontology and his dig site manager in Montana.

While the group searched for Eric, Brennan came across a raptor's nest in the jungle. He knew that raptor eggs were worth a lot of money—money that could keep the dig site going for many years. So Brennan grabbed two of them and put them in his backpack without telling anyone.

Eric was alive and well on Isla Sorna, living in an overturned water truck. He had survived on packaged food left behind at InGen's laboratory. Eric avoided small dinosaurs by leaving traces of large-dinosaur pee, which scared them off. He avoided large dinosaurs with the help of smoke bombs.

After finding Eric, the group stumbled into the Aviary where the pteranodons lived. One of the flying reptiles swooped down and grabbed Eric. It carried the boy away to feed to its young. Brennan flew in on a parasail and saved the teen, but soon he himself was cornered by pteranodons.

The group faced other dangers, too, including a massive spinosaurus (say: SPY-no-SORE-us) and several raptors. *Spinosaurus* was the largest of the carnivorous, which means meat-eating, dinosaurs. It was even bigger than a *T. rex*! Indeed, the spinosaurus in *Jurassic Park III* killed a *T. rex* in a ferocious battle.

Then the raptors arrived, in search of their eggs in Brennan's backpack. When Dr. Grant realized why the raptors were chasing them, he was angry and confronted his research associate. Brennan explained that he stole the eggs with the best intentions. "Some of the worst things imaginable were done with the best intentions," Grant said.

It was only after the group escaped a scary confrontation with the spinosaurus that they were all rescued by the United States Navy and the Marine Corps. That rescue included the injured Brennan. He returned to the mainland without the eggs—which had been returned to the adult raptors—but with his life.

CHAPTER 6
More Teeth

It was fourteen years before movie fans got to see the fourth installment in the film franchise, *Jurassic World*, which was released in 2015. And in the fictional universe of Jurassic Park, a lot was going on.

The biggest development was the opening of the theme park called Jurassic World. Although the original Jurassic Park attraction had never been opened to the public, the new theme park was launched in 2005 on its former site on Isla Nublar. It was rebranded with the name Jurassic World. The owner was no longer InGen Corporation, but another company, Masrani Global Corporation, headed by Simon Masrani, one of the world's ten richest people. Masrani had bought the company in 1998 from Dr. John Hammond.

MASRANI

Masrani Global built a first-class theme park and resort on Isla Nublar. It had everything visitors could want or need. As soon as guests arrived at the Visitor Center, they were greeted by a huge display board that outlined activities all over the island—even Jurassic Tennis!

At the Innovation Center, kids could search for dinosaur fossils at a dig site. Or they might create full-size hologram images of a dinosaur with the high-tech Holoscape. At the Petting Zoo, they could get close to, and even ride, small dinosaurs. During the day, guests had access to gift shops and food concessions. At night, they stayed in a fancy hotel.

Masrani Global Corporation also spared no expense on security. It used the latest engineering equipment and technology to make sure the more than twenty thousand visitors who crowded the island were safe from dangerous dinosaurs—or so Masrani thought.

Everything seemed to be going well. Visitors to Jurassic World were happy. The park was making lots of money for Masrani Global. But the company wanted to make the park even more thrilling for visitors. At first, when Jurassic World opened, it was a huge deal for people to see real live dinosaurs—to view them up close, and even to touch them. But after ten years, the excitement was wearing off. Seeing a dinosaur was no longer as thrilling as it had once been.

At least that's the way Claire Dearing saw it. "These days, kids look at a stegosaurus like an elephant from the city zoo," she said. The actress

Bryce Dallas Howard starred as Claire Dearing, the woman hired by Masrani to manage his park. She was all business, concerned only with making sure that Jurassic World was earning money for her employer. Dearing was so focused on work that she didn't even make time to spend with her nephews, teenaged Zach and his younger brother, Gray, who came to visit the park.

Claire Dearing viewed the dinosaurs at Jurassic World strictly as exciting attractions.

Echo, Charlie, Delta, and Blue

One person who didn't agree with that opinion was Owen Grady, a former Navy Seal turned animal behaviorist. Grady, played by Chris Pratt, was hired to train a group of young raptors at Jurassic World, named Echo, Delta, Charlie, and Blue. He had a special bond with Blue.

To generate more interest in Jurassic World, Dearing and Masrani believed the park needed a dinosaur that was bigger and scarier. They needed a dinosaur that, in Dearing's words, had "more teeth." So they brought on genetic biologist Dr. Henry Wu, the scientist who engineered the creation of the dinosaurs at Jurassic Park and Jurassic World.

To make a dinosaur bigger, scarier, and with more teeth than ever before, Dr. Wu created a hybrid dinosaur from several different ones.

They included *T. rex*, *Giganotosaurus* (say: gig-ahn-oh-toe-SORE-us), *Velociraptor*, and others. He also used some genes from modern animals such as cuttlefish and tree frogs. The result was fearsome—*Indominus rex* (say: in-DOM-in-us REX).

Indominus rex

The genetic mix of *Indominus rex* created all sorts of problems for Jurassic World. Not only was it larger and more aggressive than other

dinosaurs, but because of the cuttlefish genes, it could disguise itself. Because of the tree frog genes, it could vary its heat output. Because of its *Velociraptor* genes, it could communicate with raptors.

Right away, Owen Grady realized this would lead to trouble. He warned Dearing that the *Indominus rex* was dangerous. He told Masrani to destroy the animal. He knew, too, that Vic Hoskins, who was in charge of the park's security forces, wanted to use Jurassic World's fiercest dinosaurs as fighters on the battlefields of war.

Dr. Wu had never considered his dinosaurs would be anything but attractions at a theme park.

Grady was right. The park's *Indominus rex* used the specialized features of its design to escape from its paddock. The dinosaur, once on the loose and terrifying the island, soon crossed paths with Zach and Gray. They had taken their Gyrosphere—a vehicle shaped like a glass ball in which visitors toured parts of the park—into a restricted area, a place they weren't supposed to be. The *Indominus rex* crushed the Gyrosphere, sending the boys running for their lives.

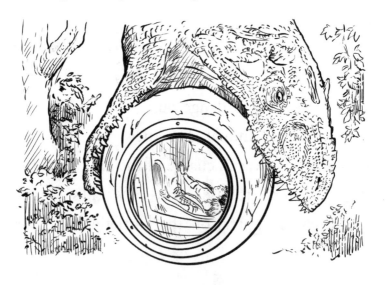

With her nephews in trouble, Dearing set out to search for them with Grady. When she saw an apatosaurus (say: a-PAT-oh-SORE-us) dying from an attack by the *Indominus rex*, her view of Jurassic World's dinosaurs changed. She realized they were not just park assets but real animals. And some of them were in trouble.

The boys escaped the *Indominus rex* with a spectacular leap over a waterfall. They managed to splash safely into the water below, but the dinosaur was still on the loose. Simon Masrani

decided the only solution was to fly a helicopter
over the *Indominus rex* and have his security forces
shoot it. The animal, however, had already crossed
the park to the Aviary. A sleek, glass building in

Jurassic World, the structure housed the park's flying reptiles. But the *Indominus rex* crashed through its glass walls, terrifying the animals inside and sending them flying into the park.

Some of the huge pteranodons attacked Masrani's helicopter, putting it into a whirling dive that ended in a fiery crash in the Aviary and killing everyone aboard.

The *Indominus rex* finally met its death after

a brutal fight with a *T. rex* and several raptors, including Blue. The battle ended when a mosasaur (say: MOH-suh-SORE) rose from the Jurassic World Lagoon to devour the hybrid dinosaur.

Jurassic World was another blockbuster movie

for Universal Pictures. Although it cost about $150 million to make, it earned more than that in box-office receipts on its first weekend alone in the United States and Canada. It has since gone on to take in more than $1.6 billion around the world. That's the seventh-highest total of any movie ever!

CHAPTER 7
Welcome to Jurassic World

The catastrophic events in the movie *Jurassic World* cost the Masrani Global Corporation hundreds of millions of dollars in lawsuits and closed the theme park Jurassic World for good. But a new problem emerged in the film *Jurassic World: Fallen Kingdom*, which was released in 2018. Mount Sibo, a volcano on Isla Nublar, was about to erupt, and the blast was expected to wipe out life on the island. That raised a huge question: Should dinosaurs be protected like other endangered species on Earth, or instead allowed to become extinct again?

For the most part, the first four movies in the Jurassic franchise took place on the remote Central American islands of Isla Nublar and Isla Sorna. Dinosaurs remained something to be observed (usually) from a distance. But the trouble that surfaced in *Jurassic World: Fallen Kingdom* was different from the perils in the previous movies. It threatened to bring dinosaurs directly to the United States mainland and into humans' everyday lives.

If the decision was made to protect the dinosaurs, then what should be done with those still living on Isla Nublar? The great asteroid that crashed into Earth sixty-five million years ago set in motion a series of deadly events. Now, with

Mount Sibo about to erupt in *Jurassic World: Fallen Kingdom*, should humans do nothing while another force of nature destroys the non-avian dinosaur population? Or should they step in and try to rescue the dinosaurs?

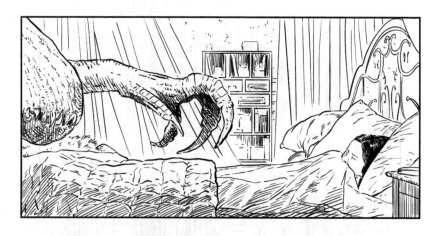

On one side of the debate was the United States Senate, which decided that it was best to let nature run its course. Dr. Ian Malcolm of the earlier Jurassic movies testified to the US Senate about how dangerous it was for human beings to interfere with the course of nature. Malcolm had warned Dr. John Hammond about that very

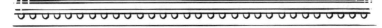
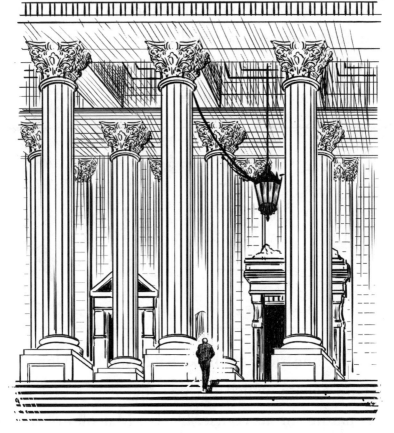

idea in the original Jurassic Park movie. Now, he warned the US government that if it stopped the second extinction of dinosaurs, humans would surely suffer.

On the other side of the debate was Claire Dearing and the Dinosaur Protection Group (DPG). Dearing—the former operations manager of Jurassic World who once thought of dinosaurs only as park attractions—founded the DPG after the Costa Rican government announced that Mount Sibo was active for the first time in almost five hundred years.

The DPG

According to the Dinosaur Protection Group website—yes, the organization really does have an actual website!—the organization was founded in 2017. It is "dedicated to establishing and protecting the rights of all living dinosaurs. The DPG operates under the principle that dinosaurs are not ours to experiment upon or exploit for entertainment or financial gain. Though we brought them back to existence, we do not thereby claim the right to assume control of them."

Visitors to the official website (www.dinosaurprotectiongroup.com) can watch a video of Claire Dearing interacting with children, learn about Mount Sibo and the dangers it presented, and even "adopt a dino."

"We are focused upon securing [dinosaurs'] health, providing a sustainable environment, and limiting human intrusion into their lives," the site notes.

Lockwood Manor

Sir Benjamin Lockwood, a former partner of Jurassic Park founder Dr. John Hammond, lived on an estate in Northern California with his granddaughter, Maisie. Lockwood contacted the DPG and offered another remote island as a sanctuary if Claire Dearing could have the dinosaurs transported there. That meant she and her team had to go to Isla Nublar themselves. She asked Owen Grady, the former Navy Seal who trained raptors at Jurassic World, to help.

Grady wanted no part of it at first. "A rescue op to save the dinosaurs from an island that's about to explode," he said sarcastically. "What could go wrong?" However, he changed his mind after watching an old video of him training the raptor Blue. He knew Blue and the other dinosaurs needed his help.

Of course, it wouldn't be a Jurassic World movie if there weren't complications. Dearing and Grady barely escaped from Isla Nublar before the erupting Mount Sibo destroyed the island. Then they discovered that Eli Mills, Lockwood's assistant who was in charge of his money, had his own idea about what to do with the dinosaurs. He hired an elite group that intended to capture the most dangerous dinosaurs and sell them to the highest bidder. He also hired Dr. Wu to create another crossbreed hybrid called an *Indoraptor*. It was the deadliest hybrid ever—a combination of an *Indominus rex* and a *Velociraptor*.

Mills and his group secretly brought the dinosaurs from Isla Nublar, including Blue, to Lockwood's estate in Northern California. Mills wasn't about to let anyone stand in the way of

his plan—not even Lockwood, whom he killed.

Dearing and Grady tried to free the dinosaurs on the estate. Grady managed to break up the auction where the dinosaurs were being sold,

but the *Indoraptor* broke out of his cage and went on a rampage, killing several people before being destroyed in a fight with Blue.

The other dinosaurs broke out of their holding areas, only to be trapped in the basement of the estate, where poison gas threatened to kill them all. Grady convinced Dearing that it was too dangerous to free the animals, but Maisie felt different about it. Only minutes earlier, she had discovered that she wasn't really Lockwood's granddaughter after all. Instead, she had been genetically made, too. So she pushed a button, opening a door that allowed the dinosaurs to leave the enclosed grounds of the estate. Why did she free the dinosaurs? "They're alive," she explained, "like me."

Blue and the other dinosaurs fled into the Northern California countryside. Their escape brought about the reality that Dr. Malcolm had warned of in his testimony before the US Senate: a world where humans and dinosaurs would be thrown together in the same environment.

Blue

CHAPTER 8
The Story Continues

The sixth movie in the series, *Jurassic World Dominion*, reached theaters in June 2022. It brought together many of the central characters in the preceding films, including Drs. Sattler, Grant, Malcolm, and Wu, as well as Claire Dearing, Owen Grady, and Maisie Lockwood—plus, dinosaurs old and new. The movie raised

the exciting, but terrifying, idea of dinosaurs living in our world.

Jurassic World Dominion also introduced the scary prospect of giant locusts that threatened the global food supply. Locusts are large grasshoppers that sometimes fly together in huge swarms. They eat plants and can do much damage to crops. But the locusts in *Jurassic World Dominion* were a type that had been extinct since the Cretaceous Period. They were engineered by Dr. Wu for Lewis Dodgson and his genetics company, Biosyn. Dodgson last appeared in the original *Jurassic Park* movie, trying to illegally buy dinosaur embryos from Dennis Nedry.

Sattler and Grant were on hand in *Jurassic World Dominion* to uncover the reason the locusts were created. They were helped by Malcolm, who was working for Biosyn but suspected the company was up to something evil. It wanted to dominate the world's food supply, and its locusts were getting out of control.

Meanwhile, Dearing, Grady, and Maisie were living in a cabin in the Sierra Nevada Mountains in California. Biosyn hired poachers to kidnap Maisie and a young female raptor that was born to Blue. Dr. Wu needed information from their genes to modify those in the locusts. He saw the danger the locusts had become and wanted to undo the damage.

In their efforts to rescue Maisie and the young raptor named Beta, Dearing and Grady

Beta

eventually learned that they had been taken to Biosyn's headquarters in Italy in a cargo plane. A pilot named Kayla Watts had taken them there, and she wanted to help rescue Maisie.

After many frightening adventures with dinosaurs in the Biosyn Valley, Grady and Dearing found Maisie, along with Grant, Sattler, and Malcolm, who were all trying to escape with the evidence they needed to prove Biosyn was up to no good. But just as they were reunited, they encountered more dangerous dinosaurs,

Giganotosaurus

including a *Giganotosaurus*, the biggest land carnivore dinosaur yet. "Bigger—why do they always have to go bigger?" Dr. Malcolm wearily asked.

After a dramatic escape, the group is flown to safety by Kayla Watts. Although her plane was destroyed, she was able to fly them all out of the valley in one of the Biosyn helicopters.

Drs. Sattler, Grant, Malcolm, and Wu were safe; Maisie was back with Dearing and Grady; and Beta was reunited with her mother, Blue.

Dodgson did not survive. Fittingly, he was killed by a dilophosaur—the same type of dinosaur that killed Dennis Nedry in *Jurassic Park*.

Jurassic World Dominion gave fans another thrilling chapter in the Jurassic World story. Since the initial *Jurassic Park* movie in 1993, the Jurassic World franchise has become to the movies what dinosaurs were to the earth some 150 million-plus years ago: dominant.

Fans can always find a way to be a part of the Jurassic franchise. Want to read more about Claire Dearing, the former operations manager at Jurassic World turned dinosaur conservationist? You can discover her backstory in a book, *The Evolution of Claire*. Want to learn more about the age of dinosaurs? Check out Jurassic World: The Exhibition. Want to feel what it's like to get up close to a velociraptor? Visit Universal Studios Hollywood's Raptor Encounter.

Raptor Encounter

In addition to the Jurassic Park and Jurassic World movies, fans can also watch the animated series *Jurassic World: Camp Cretaceous.*

Jurassic World rides and attractions are featured in the United States at Universal Studios Hollywood in California, Universal's Islands of Adventure in Florida, and beyond at Universal Studios Japan, and Universal Beijing Resort.

Spinoff books, video games, toys, and more are all part of the total Jurassic World experience.

The film franchise made movie history for the innovative way it brought CGI to moviemaking. It also made moviegoers think about important topics. Have human beings gone too far interfering with nature? Do man-made creatures have animal rights? And just because human beings *can* do something, does that mean they *should*?

Off the screen, the franchise fueled renewed interest in dinosaurs and in paleontology—so much so that it led many museums around the world to update their dinosaur exhibits. After all, they had to meet the expectations of people who had seen and loved the movies.

Colin Trevorrow, the director of *Jurassic World* and *Jurassic World Dominion* once said he wanted to showcase a theme park that kids would ask their parents to take them to. Jurassic World, with its live dinosaurs, is not and never was, of course, a real theme park. But through the movies, Jurassic World is still a place we can all visit, and enjoy, over and over again.

Bibliography

*Books for young readers

Conan Doyle, Arthur. *The Lost World*. Seattle: AmazonClassics, 2017.

Crichton, Michael. *Jurassic Park*. New York: Alfred A. Knopf, 1990.

Crichton, Michael. *The Lost World*. New York: Alfred A. Knopf, 1995.

*Lambert, David. *Dinosaur*. New York: DK Publishing, 2014.

Mitchell, W. J. T. *The Last Dinosaur Book: The Life and Times of a Cultural Icon*. Chicago: University of Chicago Press, 1998.

*Stine, Megan. *What Was the Age of the Dinosaurs?* New York: Grosset & Dunlap, 2017.

*Woodward, John. *Dinosaur!* New York: DK Publishing, 2019.

Timeline of Jurassic World

1905 | **1912** | **1990** | **1993** | **1995** | **1996** | **1997** | **2001** | **2015** | **2018** | **2020** | **2022**

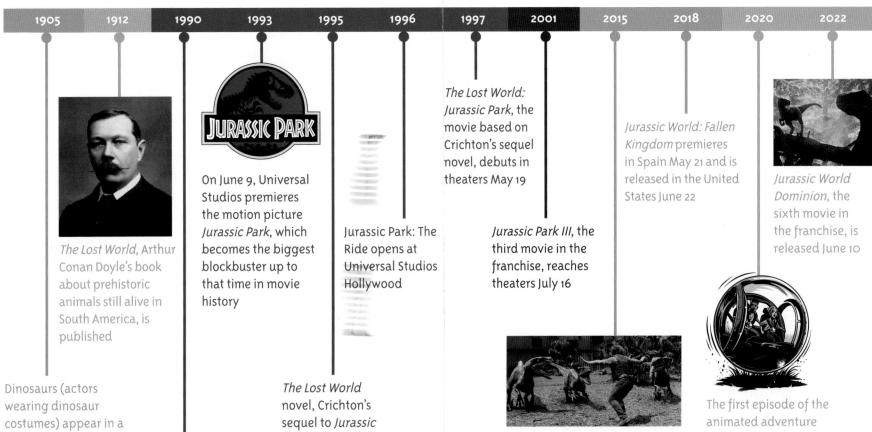

The Lost World, Arthur Conan Doyle's book about prehistoric animals still alive in South America, is published

On June 9, Universal Studios premieres the motion picture *Jurassic Park*, which becomes the biggest blockbuster up to that time in movie history

Jurassic Park: The Ride opens at Universal Studios Hollywood

The Lost World: Jurassic Park, the movie based on Crichton's sequel novel, debuts in theaters May 19

Jurassic Park III, the third movie in the franchise, reaches theaters July 16

Jurassic World: Fallen Kingdom premieres in Spain May 21 and is released in the United States June 22

Jurassic World Dominion, the sixth movie in the franchise, is released June 10

Dinosaurs (actors wearing dinosaur costumes) appear in a movie for the first time in *Prehistoric Peeps*

Michael Crichton's book *Jurassic Park* is published and becomes a best seller

The Lost World novel, Crichton's sequel to *Jurassic Park*, is published

Jurassic World, the fourth movie in the franchise, premieres June 9

The first episode of the animated adventure series *Jurassic World: Camp Cretaceous* is shown on Netflix September 18